ONE UP AND ONE TO GO

A nostalgic look at classic Scottish golf

by Stuart Marshall

First published in the United Kingdom 1997.
by Stenlake Publishing, Ochiltree Sawmill, The Lade,
Ochiltree, Ayrshire KA18 2NX.
© Stuart Marshall 1997

ISBN 1 84033 017 1

FORE! word

Scotland is the Home of Golf. Living in Scotland we can play on most of the famous courses just by paying a small fee, courses that have a history, tradition and character all of their own. As an avid collector of old golf postcards and cigarette cards I can travel back to the past and be Herd or Sayers with Old Tom looking over my shoulder. And I can dream too of winning the Open in the year 2000 at St Andrews – see you there on the winner's rostrum.

The author would like to thank Mr M. Foggo for his help with this book.

An Alphabet of St. Andrews

An interesting composition by the late Professor Crum Brown has been sent to us by a correspondent who is a keen student of the lore and literature of the game. Professorial golf has been, not with uniform fairness, summed up in the caddie's famous comment to the man of the Chair, " It tak's a heid to play gowff." Our correspondent reminds us that Professor Crum Brown was not a golfer " even in the limited professorial sense of the term, but he enjoyed great distinction at St. Andrews as the uncle of Freddy Tait."
Scotsman, 10th March, 1925.

A was his Attitude at the first tee.
B was the Burn he got into in three.
C was his Caddie, a little scapegrace.
D was the Divot he didn't replace.
E was the Energy rashly bestowed.
F was the Fore ! he roared out of the road.
G was the Globe that he missed with his putter ;
H was a Horrid word they heard him utter.
I was the Iron he used at the dyke ;
J was the Jerk laid him dead in the like.
K was a Kick knocked him into the nose ;
L was his Language which you may suppose,
M was his Mashie, he thought it would do ;
N was the Niblick he had to take too.
O was the Odd he played out of a whin.
P was a Putt he got cleverly in.
Q was a Quarrel arose unforseen, whether
R was or was not a Rub of the green.
S was a Stymie complete as could be ;
T was the Twist with which round it went he.
U was the Underspin makes the ball so⸱⸱
V was the Velocity it should b⸱⸱
W was Walkinshaw. he (thought b⸱ ⸱⸱⸱ it ;
X was the E⸱⸱
Y was the Y⸱
Z was the Zi⸱⸱
&c. Then con⸱ round.
You wo⸱ ⸱ound.

This page and opposite: group photographs at St Cuthbert's, Prestwick circa 1910.

Old St Cuthbert's was famous for the Pow Burn which ran through it and where children liked to play.

The Pleasures of Prestwick 25/7/04.

It's said that you never see the greens at Prestwick until you are on them, which is usually eight or ten strokes after teeing off!

Prestwick Golf Club was founded in 1851 with Lord Eglinton as its first captain. In 1853 Tom Morris was appointed greenkeeper for the princely sum of £25 per year.

Prime Minister & Home Secretary on the Golf Links, Prestwick. 432

The land here once belonged to the Abbey of Paisley. Legend has it that the Cardinal's Nob, an infamous hazard, got its name when the Monk of Crossraguel lost his nose in a wager over a game of golf here.

The first Open, held at Prestwick in 1860, was won by Willie Park. In 1861, the championship became truly *open* when amateurs were admitted. A stone cairn marks the spot where the original first tee was sited.

At the 9th Hole, Golf Links, Prestwick.   433

In the 1920s, a short walk would take members from this hole to the Royal Troon
course, playing out from one course and back from the other later in the day.

Harold Hilton won the Amateur Championship at Prestwick in 1911. E A Lassen was the runner-up.

Another view of the 1911 Amateur Championship Final. Three months later Hilton added the American title at Apawamis, New York.

Ladies St. Nicholas Golf Course, Prestwick.

Mary, Queen of Scots, was supposedly a keen golfer. As far back as 1774, the Royal Musselburgh
Golf Club had a tournament for ladies and in 1867 St Andrews Ladies Golf Club was founded.

St. Nicholas Golf Course, Prestwick.

In 1864 the Committee decided to gather in all the medals and trophies belonging to the club and a case to display them in was provided . In 1902 Alex Herd, the Open champion, played here and won against David Kinnell, the club professional, using a revolutionary new ball, the Haskell.

How these ladies at St Nicholas' managed to play with their stiff collars, long skirts and hats amazes me.

3RD HOLE, ST. NICHOLAS GOLF LINKS, PRESTWICK.

657

Players on St Nicholas' often have to contend with a stiff breeze blowing in from the sea!

Above are G. Lockhart, J. Robb, Bobbie Andrew and J. Thomson. This postcard dates from 1911, the year that Andrew left to become the professional at Newhaven County Golf Club, New York. A contest was held to bid farewell to him and prior to it these four played an exhibition game. Andrew held the amateur record (69) for many years and represented Scotland six times from 1905 to 1910.

In June 1907, while playing at Troon, Bobbie Andrew found his ball impaled by a hairpin. The hole cost him ten strokes and he lost the competition, the Hillhouse Cup, by two strokes. Only later was he told that he could have removed the pin without penalty.

A.J. Balfour was captain of North Berwick from 1891 to 1892. He went on to become Prime Minister.

MUNICIPAL GOLF CLUB HOUSE, PRESTWICK.

A postcard produced around 1905 of the municipal golf clubhouse at Prestwick. Long gone, it was situated near today's ice rink at Prestwick Toll.

290
GOLF CLUB HOUSE AND MARINE HOTEL, TROON

The first Open at Troon was in 1923 and was won by Arthur Havers with an aggregate score of 295. The course possibly witnessed one of the great Open shots when in 1973 Gene Sarazen holed the Postage Stamp (8th hole) in one.

Troon Municipal Golf Course, The Warren

Although Troon is noted for its Royal Golf Club, there are also three municipal courses – Darley, Fullarton and Lochgreen, the latter of which has been used as a qualifying course for the Open.

Initially a course at Turnberry was constructed by the Marquis of Ailsa. In 1902 Turnberry Golf Club was formed and in 1906 the hotel was opened by the Glasgow & South Western Railway Company. During both world wars an airfield was used at Turnberry. Between the wars the hotel and course were frequented by the rich and famous. The Ailsa course was rebuilt after World War II and since re-opening in 1951 has been one of the world's leading courses.

Barassie Golf Club House

Situated to the north of Troon, Barassie's clubhouse was designed and built by traders from Kilmarnock in 1877.

Rothesay Golf Course, showing Loch Ascog and Loch Fad.

Opened in 1892, Rothesay is renowned for its views of the surrounding sea and hills. It is one of three courses on the Isle of Bute, the others being Kingarth and Port Bannatyne

The Golf Clubhouse, Millport about 1906.

STARTING TEE AND SHELTER, MONTROSE GOLF COURSE

Montrose has a long golfing history. Little has changed there since 1863 when it was extended to 18 holes from the original Medal Course of 17 holes.

The First Tee at Montrose around 1906 – I wonder if the little girl was used as a caddie. The original land was owned by the Earl of Dalhousie and has been home to different clubs including North Links Ladies, Caledonia Golf Club, the Mercantile Golf Club, the Victoria Golf Club and the Royal Albert.

1682

ON THE 6TH GREEN, DUNBAR GOLF COURSE.

Dunbar Golf Course is one of the finest links in Scotland. In 1946 J. H. Taylor presented the club
with a document titled 'The Regulations of the Dunbar Golfing Society, 14th May 1794'.

North Berwick from Point Garry

Founded in 1832, North Berwick Club can claim to be one of the oldest.

Innerleven and Thistle Golf Club Houses, Leven

The Leven Golfing Society was formed in 1820. The original links were divided into the Leven and Lundin Links in 1869.

Golf Links, Leven

Leven is best remembered for its 18th hole, a par four of 457 yards which finishes directly in front of its majestic clubhouse.

Carnoustie Course, established in 1842, is famous for its Barry Burn finish. It has
the honour of being the venue for the last Open of the century in July 1999.

Ben Hogan won his one and only British Open at Carnoustie in 1953 with a total score of 282.
Before he won he commented "I've got a lawnmower back in Texas. I'll send it over".

This postcard of the links at Carnoustie was published in 1904. The sender has marked with a cross the house where he was staying.

Nobody knows when golf was first played at St Andrews, but the game was popular when the University was founded in 1413. Old Tom Morris is standing in the foreground of this picture.

H.R.H. THE PRINCE OF WALES AT ST. ANDREWS.
"PLAYING HIMSELF IN" AS CAPTAIN OF THE R. & A. GOLF CLUB.

"DUNDEE ADVERTISER" PHOTO.

The first royal patron of St Andrews was King William IV in 1834 and thereafter the club became the 'Royal and Ancient Golf Club of St Andrews'. Edward VII, while Prince of Wales, was the first royal captain. The above Prince of Wales (later Edward VIII) was an active captain and was so popular that he was made a Freeman of the City. Here he is pictured in 1922 before a crowd of over 7000.

St. Andrews. On the 4th Hole Green. Length of Hole 385 yds. (4 Hole)

Little has changed of the Old Course over the last few centuries. Originally the course was over 22 holes; the present day 18 is due in no small instance to a William St Clair who in 1764 took 121 strokes to cover the links. The Society of St Andrews ' Golfers (later to be the R.&.A.) formed 10 years earlier deemed this an act of sacrilege, hence leading to the change in the course to 18 holes.

Tom Morris.   Harry Vardon   Alexr. Herd (Champion 1902).

Open Championship.

Harry Vardon (1870 – 1937) won the British Open six times and the U.S. Open once. This 1900 picture shows Tom Morris keeping an eye on the youngsters.

Open Championship.—J. H. Taylor driving.

Famous Golfers. Valentines Series

John Henry Taylor won the Open five times. Tom Morris once more keeps watch as he drives off at St Andrews.

Medal Play.—The late Mr F. G. Tait driving.

Famous Golfers.   Valentines Series

Freddie Tait was killed in action during the Boer War in February 1900, aged 30. He was Amateur Champion in 1896 and 1898.

Golfing — Among the Whins

At one time grazing sheep and rabbits kept the grass short on the course, but they only nibbled at the whins!

Golfing — A Disputed Shot

When o'er this trackless moor
you're Played,
Where'er the ball doth roam,
your thoughts will soon not be on Golf,
But on returning home.

Ed Furgol, an American professional, once said, 'There's nothing wrong with St Andrews that a hundred bulldozers couldn't put right'.

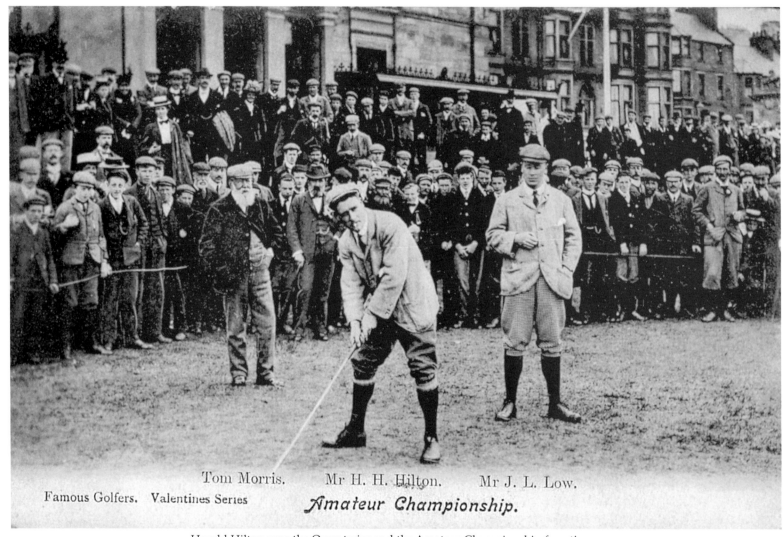

Tom Morris.   Mr H. H. Hilton.   Mr J. L. Low.

Famous Golfers.   Valentines Series

Amateur Championship.

Harold Hilton won the Open twice and the Amateur Championship four times.

Golfing.—"The Swing"

Will be down with the 6.15 from St. Enoch's same as B.S. J.F.McF.

This postcard from the turn of the century epitomises Sir Walter Simpson's maxim, expressed in his 1897 *The Art of Golf* – 'There is one essential only in the golf swing, the ball must be hit.'

Golfing — The Swing

If your swing isn't right the Old Course will find you out!

Golfing — In a Bunker

St. Andrews.

When in a Bunker, don't despair,
Wield well your club. Ball flies in air. youfer.

Sam Snead on first seeing St Andrews said, 'Say, that looks like an old abandoned golf course. What do they call it?'

As Peter Alliss said "It's sickening to drive dead straight and see some fairway hump divert the ball into a bunker."

Alex. Herd (Champion).   Andrew Kirkcaldy.

Open Championship.

Famous Golfers.   Valentines Series

Alex Herd won his only Open at Hoylake in 1902 with a one-shot victory over Vardon and Braid. This picture was possibly taken at the 1900 Open at St Andrews which was won by J. H. Taylor. Andrew Kirkaldy went on to serve as the club professional from 1910 to 1933.

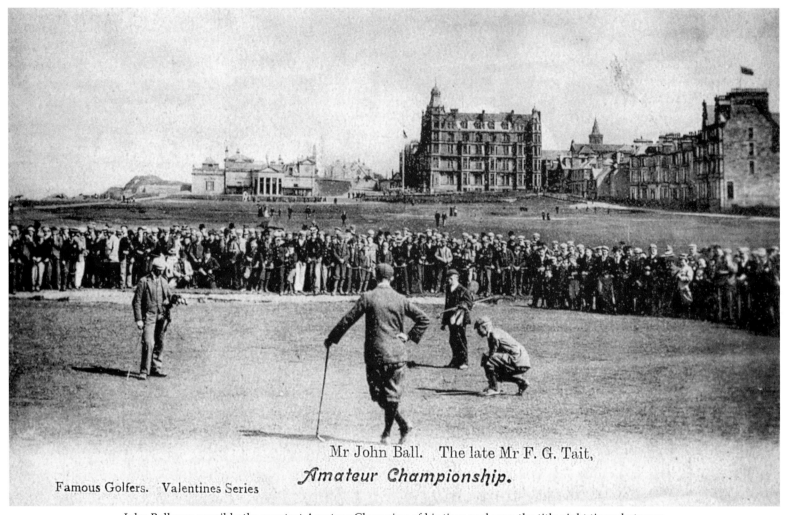

Mr John Ball.   The late Mr F. G. Tait,
Amateur Championship.

Famous Golfers.   Valentines Series

John Ball was possibly the greatest Amateur Champion of his time and won the title eight times between 1888 and 1912. He was the first amateur to win the Open Championship, a feat he achieved in 1890.

Foursome Match for £200—KIRKCALDY and HERD v. SAYERS and SIMPSON.

Archie Simpson.   Alexr. Herd.

Andrew Kirkcaldy.

BenSayers.

The prize money of £200 may be small beer by today's standards but was a fortune for the working man in the early years of the century.

Mr Leslie Balfour Melville winning Medal. (Record score—78.)

Famous Golfers. Valentine's Series

Leslie Balfour Melville had over thirty R. & A. wins, starting with the Club Gold Medal in 1874 and ending with the Club Gold and the George Glennie Medals, both of which he won in 1908. His only British Amateur Championship victory came in 1895 when he won at the 19th hole over J. Ball.

Thomas Morris (1821 – 1908), known as Old Tom, was one of the world's greatest golfers. He started playing golf at six years old and as a caddie was apprenticed to the famous golfer, Sandy Robertson. Often considered to be the first course designer, his skills in laying out courses were sought after throughout Britain.

L to R, Top: A. Herd (1868 – 1944), J. H. Taylor (1871 – 1963)
Bottom: J. Braid (1870 – 1950), H. Vardon (1870 – 1937)

1. W. Fernie.
2. H. Vardon.
3. J. Braid.
4. J. Taylor.
5. C. H. Mayo.
6. A. Simpson.
7. J. White.
8. A. Herd.
9. A. Kirkaldy.
10. B. Sayers, Junr.
11. J. H. Taylor.
12. A. Massey.
13. G. Duncan.

Some of the greatest golfers ever known.